Contents

Some words are printed in bold, **like this**. You can find out what they mean in the glossary.

Do you know someone with diabetes?

You might have a friend with diabetes mellitus, often just called 'diabetes'. Diabetes is a **medical condition**. This means that the doctor has given your friend things to do to stay healthy.

You cannot catch diabetes.

I Know Someone with
Diabetes

Vic Parker

www.raintreepublishers.co.uk
Visit our website to find out
more information about
Raintree books.

To order:

☎ Phone 0845 6044371

🖷 Fax +44 (0) 1865 312263

✉ Email myorders@raintreepublishers.co.uk

Customers from outside the UK please telephone +44 1865 312262

Raintree is an imprint of Capstone Global Library Limited,
a company incorporated in England and Wales having
its registered office at 7 Pilgrim Street, London, EC4V 6LB –
Registered company number: 6695582

Text © Capstone Global Library Limited 2011
First published in hardback in 2011
First published in paperback in 2012
The moral rights of the proprietor have been asserted.

Edited by Rebecca Rissman, Daniel Nunn
  and Siân Smith
Designed by Joanna Hinton Malivoire
Picture research by Mica Brancic
Originated by Capstone Global Library
Printed and bound in China by Leo Paper Products Ltd

ISBN 978 1 406 22076 6 (hardback)
15 14 13 12 11
10 9 8 7 6 5 4 3 2 1

ISBN 978 1 406 22349 1 (paperback)
16 15 14 13 12 11
10 9 8 7 6 5 4 3 2 1

British Library Cataloguing in Publication Data
Parker, Victoria.
I know someone with diabetes. – (Understanding health
issues)
  1. Diabetes–Juvenile literature.
  I. Title II. Series
  616.4'62-dc22

Acknowledgements
We would like to thank the following for permission to
reproduce photographs: Alamy pp. 15 (© ACE Stock
Limited), 16 (© Anne-Marie Palmer), 17 (© Martin Shields);
Getty Images pp. 18 (PhotoAlto Agency RF Collections/
Odilon Dimier), 27 (AFP Photo/Thomas Coex); Getty
Images Entertainment p. 26 (Jemal Countess); iStockphoto
pp. 6 (© Steve Debenport), 13 (© Aldo Murillo), 20 (©
Cristian Lazzari), 21 (© Christopher Futcher), 23 (© Radu
Razvan); Photolibrary pp. 4 (Radius Images), 5 (Uppercut
Images RF/Jay Reilly), 7 (Photoalto/Laurence Mouton), 8
(age fotostock/Javier Larrea), 9 (imagebroker.net/Martin
Moxter), 10 (OJO Images/Sam Edwards), 11 (Banana
Stock), 14 (BSIP Medical/May May), 19 (Index Stock
Imagery/Robert Ginn), 22 (BSIP Medical/Jose Oto), 25
(Image Source); Shutterstock p. 12 (© Maga).

Cover photograph of a couple and their daughter
cooking reproduced with permission of Getty Images
(Photodisc/Jack Hollingsworth).

We would like to thank Matthew Siegel and Ashley Wolinski
for their invaluable help in the preparation of this book.

Someone with diabetes can wear a bracelet or necklace to let others know.

You cannot tell that someone has diabetes just by looking at them. There is nothing to see. This is because diabetes happens on the inside of someone's body, not the outside.

What is Type 1 diabetes?

When we eat, our bodies make something inside us called **insulin**. Insulin helps turn the sugar we get from certain foods into **energy**, so we can run and jump and play.

Sugar comes from foods such as bread, bananas, sweets, and pasta.

Too much sugar in your blood can make you feel very tired, thirsty, and unwell.

When a young person gets Type 1 diabetes, their body stops making insulin. This means their body cannot turn sugar from their food into energy. Instead, the sugar builds up in their blood and makes them unwell.

How do you get Type 1 diabetes?

No one is sure why young people get Type 1 diabetes. Some children who develop it have an older relative with Type 1 diabetes too. Others suddenly get it after a nasty illness.

Many scientists are working to discover what causes Type 1 diabetes.

Young people with diabetes can join groups or go on breaks where they can have fun and meet other people with diabetes.

Most young people who get Type 1 diabetes are between the ages of 10 and 14. However, some are even younger. Once you get Type 1 diabetes, you have it for the rest of your life.

A different type of diabetes

Many more adults than young people get diabetes. Adults usually develop a different type of the **medical condition**. This is called Type 2 diabetes.

Many people have grandparents with Type 2 diabetes.

A person with Type 2 diabetes still makes **insulin** in their body. However, this insulin either does not work as well as it should, or there is not enough of it.

Sugar can build up in the blood of someone with Type 2 diabetes, just as it can for someone with Type 1 diabetes.

The causes of Type 2 diabetes

Exercising and eating healthily can help everyone to stay well.

Adults can get Type 2 diabetes if they are overweight. This is often because they have made unhealthy food choices and have not taken regular exercise.

Adults are more likely to get Type 2 diabetes if other people in their family have it too. People from certain **ethnic** backgrounds, such as Afro-Caribbean, South-Asian, or Hispanic, are also more likely to develop Type 2 diabetes.

You might be surprised by how many grown-ups you know who have Type 2 diabetes.

Living with Type 1 diabetes

Someone with Type 1 diabetes needs to take **insulin** as medicine. Then their body can turn the sugar from food into **energy** and they feel well. They have up to five **injections** of insulin every day.

Insulin injection needles are so small you can hardly feel them.

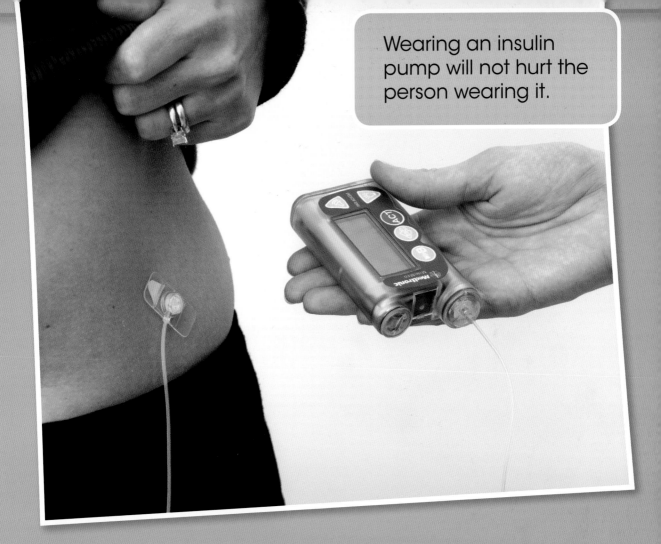

Other people with Type 1 diabetes use an insulin pump. This clips onto their clothes while a tiny needle stays in their skin. You can sleep, shower, and even swim wearing an insulin pump.

Living with Type 2 diabetes

Many people with Type 2 diabetes can take tablets as treatment. These tablets either get the body to make enough **insulin**, or help the body's insulin to work better.

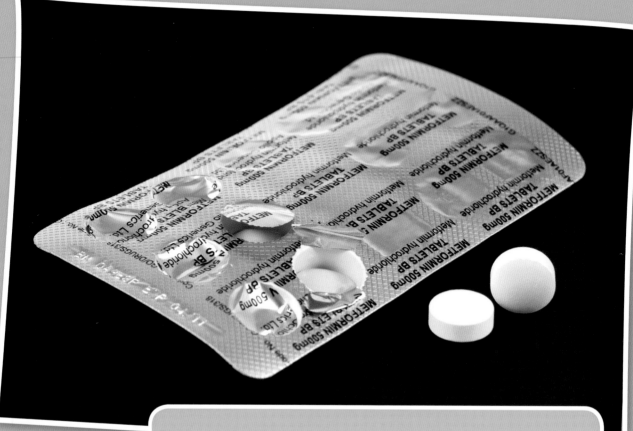

You can help a friend with Type 2 diabetes by reminding them to take their tablets.

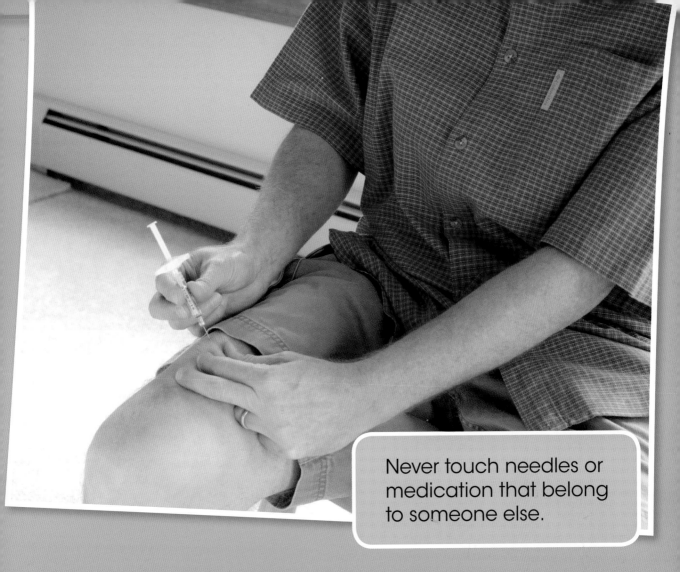

Never touch needles or medication that belong to someone else.

Some people with Type 2 diabetes have **injections**. These may be of a medicine that works the same way that tablets do. Or they may be injections of insulin.

What is a hypo?

Sometimes, someone with diabetes may turn pale, shaky, confused, and grumpy. This is because all the sugar from their food has been turned into **energy** and used up. It is called having a **hypo**.

You may realize that a friend with diabetes is having a hypo before they do.

Someone having a hypo needs a sugary drink or some sugary sweets straight away. They should soon feel better. If they do not, you can help by calling an ambulance urgently.

If someone having a hypo does not have sugar quickly enough, they may pass out and have a **seizure**.

Food choices

To stay well, people with diabetes should eat regular, small amounts of starchy food at meal and snack times. Starchy foods include potatoes, rice, pasta, and bread.

Bananas are a tasty starchy food.

We should all make healthy food choices to stay well.

People with diabetes should usually avoid sugary foods, but eat lots of vegetables and **wholefoods**. They should not skip meals or their healthy snacks. People without diabetes should also do these things to eat healthily.

About blood testing

If someone with diabetes does not follow their doctor's instructions, the amount of sugar in their blood may rise too high. This can harm different body parts, such as their eyes and **nerves**.

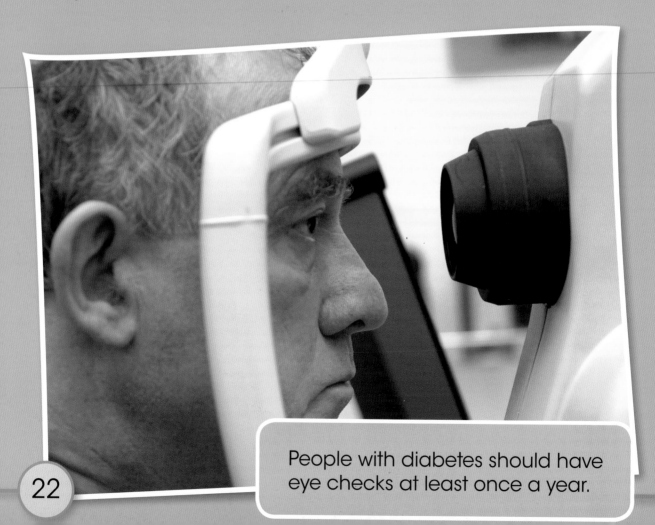

People with diabetes should have eye checks at least once a year.

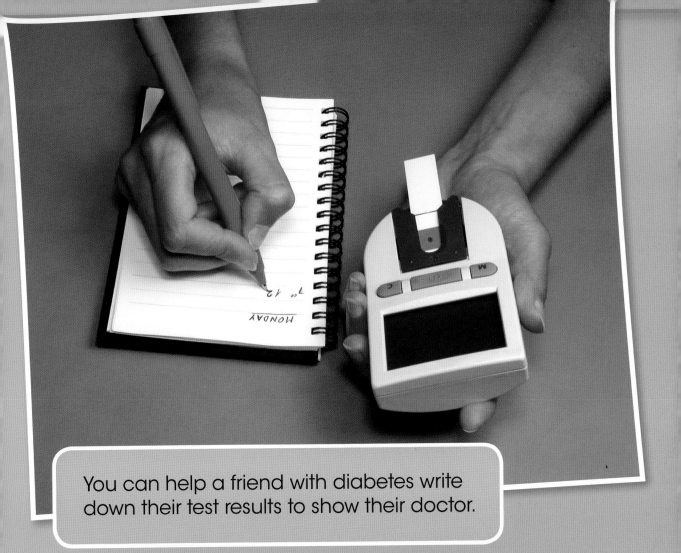

You can help a friend with diabetes write down their test results to show their doctor.

A person with diabetes can check how much sugar is in their blood by using a special machine. This can help them to keep their blood sugar level just right, so they stay healthy.

Being a good friend

There are many ways you can be a good friend to someone with diabetes. You can:

- try not to think of your friend as 'ill'

- help each other to exercise

- carry a sugary drink in case your friend has a **hypo**

- make healthy food choices with your friend.

We all have different bodies and different personalities.

Living with diabetes can be difficult at times. We are all different in many ways. A good friend likes us and values us for who we are.

Famous people with diabetes

Nick Jonas wears an **insulin** pump to manage his diabetes.

Nick Jonas got Type 1 diabetes at the age of 13. It hasn't stopped him becoming a popular singer and actor with his own TV show.

Many people say that Steve Redgrave is the greatest ever Olympic athlete.

Steve Redgrave was already a champion rower when he developed Type 1 diabetes. He worked hard to manage the **medical condition** and won gold medals at five Olympic Games!

Diabetes – facts and fiction

Facts

- At least 171 million people in the world have diabetes.

- Experts guess that half a million people have Type 2 diabetes without knowing it yet.

Fiction

(?) Eating lots of diabetic sweets and chocolate is a good idea.

> **WRONG!** 'Diabetic' foods can still raise blood sugar and can give you tummy-ache and diarrhoea.

(?) People with diabetes should never eat sugary foods and drinks.

> **WRONG!** People with diabetes may need to eat some sugary stuff at certain times, such as if they exercise, or if they are having a **hypo**.

Glossary

energy power to do something. We use energy when we run, jump, and play.

ethnic belonging to a certain race of people

hypo short for 'hypoglycaemia', which means 'low blood sugar' (not enough sugar in someone's blood)

injection people use an injection to take medicine into their bodies through a needle

insulin liquid made in our bodies which controls the amount of sugar in our blood

medical condition health problem that a person has for a long time or for life

nerves long, fine threads that carry information between body parts and the brain

seizure disturbance in someone's brain, which can affect their senses, behaviour, feelings, or thoughts for a while

wholefood food that is kept as natural as possible, without having things added or taken away from it

Find out more

Books to read

Diabetes (Feeling Ill?), Jillian Powell (Evans Brothers, 2007)

Juvenile Diabetes (First Facts), Jason Glaser (First Facts Books, 2006)

What Does it Mean to Have Diabetes?, Louise Spilsbury (Heinemann Library, 2003)

Websites

kidshealth.org/kid/centers/diabetes_center.html

Watch an animation that helps you learn about Type 1 and Type 2 diabetes on this website.

www.diabetes.org.uk/Guide-to-diabetes/Food_and_recipes

This part of the Diabetes UK's website has recipes and information on healthy eating for people who have diabetes.

Index